THESE ARE OUR BODIES

FOR MIDDLE SCHOOL

T0272725

Church Publishing
NEW YORK

PARTICIPANT BOOK

Scripture taken from the Common English Bible®, CEB® Copyright © 2010, 2011 by Common English Bible.™ Used by permission. All rights reserved worldwide. The "CEB" and "Common English Bible" trademarks are registered in the United States Patent and Trademark Office by Common English Bible. Use of either trademark requires the permission of Common English Bible.

The scripture from the *New Revised Standard Version Bible (NRSV)* © 1989 by the Division of Christian Education of the National Council of Churches of Christ in the USA. Used by permission.

Scripture quotations marked *(NLT)* are taken from the Holy Bible, *New Living Translation*, Copyright © 1996, 2004, 2007 by Tyndale House Foundation. Used by permission of Tyndale House Publishers, Inc., Carol Stream, Illinois 60188. All rights reserved.

Church Publishing Incorporated
19 East 34th Street, New York, NY 10016
www.churchpublishing.org

Cover design by Jennifer Kopec, 2 Pug Design
Typeset by Progressive Publishing Services

ISBN-13: 978-1-60674-313-3 (pbk.)
ISBN-13: 978-1-60674-314-0 (ebook)

Printed in the United States of America

CONTENTS

INTRODUCTION

Welcome to *These Are Our Bodies!*

We are so glad that you are in this program and that you have this *Participant Book*.

This book is your guide to use during each session of the program and for you to take home after the program is over. *These Are Our Bodies* is about connecting your faith life with your sexuality . . . *and that is very important and sometimes uncomfortable.* This book will help you during the program. It has prayers, scripture, and reflection questions designed to help you see the connection between your sexuality and your faith.

The book has 10 chapters, one for each session. You will use your *Participant Book* during the sessions to reflect on and record what you are thinking, feeling, and learning. We provide lots of space for you to write and doodle.

You will also find scripture passages to read and contemplate.

At the end of the book (pp. 107–119) is a Glossary. It has words that we use in the sessions and many words that are just plain good to know. Take a look—it might surprise you!

After the sessions are over, the *Participant Book* is yours to take home.

There is also a *Parent Book* for an adult in your home to use. You might want to get together and ask each other questions about what you are discovering.

Remember, this book is *YOURS!* Use it! Write in it. Keep it to recall the games you played and the things you learned.

SESSION 1

YOU ARE
GOD'S CREATION

To say that I am made in the image of God
is to say that love is the reason for my
existence, for God is love. Love is my true
identity. Selflessness is my true self. Love
is my true character. Love is my name.[1]
— Thomas Merton

....

1 Thomas Merton, *Seeds of Contemplation* (NY: New Directions Publishing Company, 1961), 46.

Holy God, one who took on flesh and lived as one of us,
dwell with us here and give us courage to learn, grow,
and become more like you—
loving, kind, and full of grace—
through God our Creator, Christ our Redeemer,
and the Spirit our Sustainer. Amen.

HOPE Ground Rules[2]

Honesty: We commit to sharing what we really think.

Openness: We commit to being open to what others say, both our group members and our leaders, and most of all to God.

Privacy: We commit to keeping what is said and done here within this space.

Enthusiasm: We commit to laughter, fun, and a sense of wonder.

Which parts of our HOPE rules are most important to you?

_____
_____
_____
_____

....

2   The authors have done their best, without success, to track down the original source of the HOPE acronym. No copyright infringement is intended. If notified, they will gladly credit the original author in future editions of *These Are Our Bodies*.

You Are GOD'S CREATION

And God saw that the light was good.
—Genesis 1:4a, *NRSV*

God called the dry land Earth, and the waters that were
gathered together he called Seas. And God saw that it
was good.
—Genesis 1:10, *NRSV*

The earth brought forth vegetation: plants yielding seed of
every kind, and trees of every kind bearing fruit with the
seed in it. And God saw that it was good.
—Genesis 1:12, *NRSV*

God set them in the dome of the sky to give light upon the
earth, to rule over the day and over the night, and to
separate the light from the darkness. And God saw that
it was good.
—Genesis 1:17–18, *NRSV*

So God created the great sea monsters and every living
creature that moves, of every kind, with which the waters
swarm, and every winged bird of every kind. And God
saw that it was good.
—Genesis 1:21, *NRSV*

God made the wild animals of the earth of every kind, and the cattle of every kind, and everything that creeps upon the ground of every kind. And God saw that it was good.

—Genesis 1:25, *NRSV*

Then God said, "Let us make humanity in our image to resemble us so that they may take charge of the fish of the sea, the birds in the sky, the livestock, all the earth, and all the crawling things on earth." God created humanity in God's own image, in the divine image God created them, male and female God created them.

—Genesis 1:26–27, *CEB*

Then God said, "Let us make humankind in our image, according to our likeness; and let them have dominion over the fish of the sea, and over the birds of the air, and over the cattle, and over all the wild animals of the earth, and over every creeping thing that creeps upon the earth. So God created humankind in his image, in the image of God he created them; male and female he created them.

—Genesis 1:26–27, *NRSV*

God saw everything that he had made, and indeed, it was very good.

—Genesis 1:31, *NRSV*

If these passages are familiar to you, upon reading them again, what do you notice now that you did not notice then? Or, if you are hearing it for the first time, what stands out from these passages?

_____

_____

_____

_____

_____

What does being made in the image of God mean to you? How does it feel to know you have been made in the image of God?

_____

_____

_____

_____

_____

Human beings are created in the image of God. The rest of creation does not have this special mark. Human beings were created to be in relationship with God.

Genesis 1:28a states, "God blessed them." Humanity was special enough to deserve a blessing! Beyond the blessing, God gave a special declaration. After creating humanity, "God saw everything that he had made, and indeed, it was very good" (Genesis 1:31a, *NRSV*). The double adjective—*very good*—is evidence of God's delight.

How does it feel to be blessed by God?

_____
_____
_____
_____
_____

The image of God is imprinted on each one of us as a part of God's creation. God views each one of us as very good. Finally, we read God's command to be fruitful and multiply in Genesis 1.

One way to be fruitful is to develop meaningful and loving relationships with others. Relationships like this require vulnerability. Vulnerability means letting others get close despite our fears or worries. It means opening ourselves up to each other, even to the parts of ourselves that we struggle to call "very good."

When you think about your friends and family, what are the most important things to you? What do you worry about? Name some of your fears. Write down some of your hopes.

_____
_____
_____
_____
_____

A Prayer for the Human Family

O God, you made us in your own image and redeemed us through Jesus your Son: Look with compassion on the whole human family; take away the arrogance and hatred which infect our hearts; break down the walls that separate us; unite us in bonds of love; and work through our struggle and confusion to accomplish your purposes on earth; that, in your good time, all nations and races may serve you in harmony around your heavenly throne; through Jesus Christ our Lord. Amen.[3]

....

3 *Book of Common Prayer*, For the Human Family, p. 814

YOU ARE
COMPLEX

You made all the delicate, inner parts of my body
and knit me together in my mother's womb.
Thank you for making me so wonderfully complex!
Your workmanship is marvelous—how well I know it.

—Psalm 139:13–14, *NLT*

Holy God, one who took on flesh and lived as one of us,
dwell with us here and give us courage to learn, grow,
and become more like you—
loving, kind, and full of grace—
through God our Creator, Christ our Redeemer,
and the Spirit our Sustainer. Amen.

You Are COMPLEX

When you looked at different pictures and thought about your feelings, what did you learn about yourself?

✏️➤ _____

_____

_____

_____

_____

What questions do you have? Write a few of your questions here.

✏️➤ _____

_____

_____

_____

_____

Gender identity, gender expression, attraction, and *biological sex* are thought by some to be *independent* of one another. All four aspects of human sexuality form in different ways and can be at different ends of a continuum. The idea of a *continuum* is one way to discuss the complexity of human sexuality.

Some new words to know:

- *Agender* refers to a person who is internally ungendered or does not feel a sense of gender identity.
- *Cisgender* refers to a person who by nature or by choice conforms to gender-based expectations of society.
- *Gender fluid* describes one who moves in and out of different ways of expressing and identifying oneself.
- *Intersex* refers to one who is born with chromosomes, external genitalia, or internal reproductive systems that do not fall into socially-constructed male and female ways of defining sex.
- *Pangender* refers to a person whose gender identity if made up of all or many gender expressions.

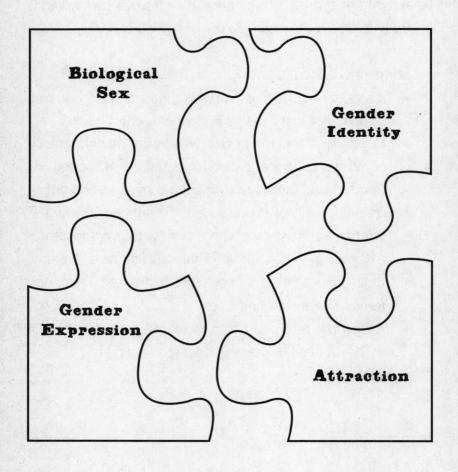

Puzzle Sheet

Write down three examples in each of the following categories:

Biological Sex

1.

_____

_____

_____

_____

2.

_____

_____

_____

_____

3.

_____

_____

_____

_____

Gender Identity

1.

_____

_____

_____

_____

_____

2.

_____

_____

_____

_____

_____

3.

_____

_____

_____

_____

_____

Gender Expression

1.

_____
_____
_____
_____
_____

2.

_____
_____
_____
_____
_____

3.

_____
_____
_____
_____
_____

Attraction

1.

_____

_____

_____

_____

_____

2.

_____

_____

_____

_____

_____

3.

_____

_____

_____

_____

_____

You are created in the image of God. Humanity, in all of its complexities, was declared "very good" by the Creator.

If you have questions about what we just covered, please write them down here. Choose one or two questions to put into the Question Box.

Think about yourself. If you speak of yourself as only "male" or "female," in what ways do you limit your viewpoint?

_____
_____
_____
_____
_____
_____

If someone only allows you to express yourself in masculine ways or in feminine ways, how well can you express your whole self?

_____
_____
_____
_____
_____
_____

Just as God is complex, so is humanity. After all, we are created in the image of God.

A Prayer for Quiet Confidence

O God of peace, who hast taught us that in returning and rest we shall be saved, in quietness and confidence shall be our strength: By the might of thy Spirit lift us, we pray thee, to thy presence, where we may be still and know that thou art God; through Jesus Christ our Lord. Amen.[4]

....

4 *Book of Common Prayer*, p. 832.

YOU ARE
ACCEPTED

Holy God, one who took on flesh and lived as one of us,
dwell with us here and give us courage to learn, grow,
and become more like you—
loving, kind, and full of grace—
through God our Creator, Christ our Redeemer,
and the Spirit our Sustainer. Amen.

Made in God's Image

The *Imago Dei* is another name for the image of God. The *Imago Dei* is hard to describe. It is hard to understand how human beings are made in the image of God.

What is the greatest *challenge* in accepting God's imprint on you? What is the greatest *comfort* in knowing you bear God's image?

Letting go of poor body image requires replacing it with an understanding of God's unconditional acceptance of us. Thinking about the images you see in magazines or in ads, why do you think advertisers use people to sell things?

What do you think the phrase *imprint of God's being* means in the passage from Hebrews?

▰▱▱▱▱▱▱▱▱▱▱▱▱▱▱▱▱▱▱▱▱▱▱▱▱▱▱▱▱▱▱▱▱▱▱▱

_____

_____

_____

How are acceptance and beauty related to sexuality? In our culture, how are they connected? In our faith, how are they connected?

▰▱▱▱▱▱▱▱▱▱▱▱▱▱▱▱▱▱▱▱▱▱▱▱▱▱▱▱▱▱▱▱▱▱▱▱

_____

_____

_____

When we watch television, read magazines, scroll through social media, and walk through the mall, advertisements overtake our senses. They consistently tell us how to define beauty in an unhealthy way. They set an unreachable standard.

God created humanity in God's own image, in the divine image God created them, male and female God created them.
—Genesis 1:27, *NRSV*

You are made in the likeness of God. Sometimes, when we accept a flawed way of thinking, we are sure to fall short. Though our *culture's* definition of beauty is flawed. God's acceptance of us is complete.

Think about your friends and family. Write a few of their names here along with what you see as beautiful in them.

_____

_____

_____

Creator God, giver of the divine image, hold us tightly within your arms of love so that even when we do not feel beautiful by the standards of the world, we are able to claim your image imprinted on us, in the name of God our life-giver, Jesus our life-redeemer, and Holy Spirit our life-perfecter. Amen.

A Prayer for Young Persons

God our Father, you see your children growing up in an unsteady and confusing world: Show them that your ways give more life than the ways of the world, and that following you is better than chasing after selfish goals. Help them to take failure, not as a measure of their worth, but as a chance for a new start. Give them strength to hold their faith in you, and to keep alive their joy in your creation, through Jesus Christ our Lord. Amen.[5]

....

5 *Book of Common Prayer*, p. 839.

YOU ARE
RELATIONAL (PART 1)

Holy God, one who took on flesh and lived as one of us,
dwell with us here and give us courage to learn, grow,
and become more like you—
loving, kind, and full of grace—
through God our Creator, Christ our Redeemer,
and the Spirit our Sustainer. Amen.

Love

Phrases to act out in the GAME:

- Love is patient
- Love is kind
- Love is not jealous
- Love does not brag
- Love is not arrogant
- Love is not rude
- Love does not seek its own advantage
- Love is not irritable
- Love does not keep a record of complaints
- Love is not happy with injustice
- Love is happy with the truth
- Love puts up with all things
- Love trusts in all things
- Love hopes for all things
- Love endures all things

First Corinthians 13:4–7 *(CEB)* offers a way to describe Christian love:

> [4]Love is patient, love is kind, it isn't jealous, it doesn't brag, it isn't arrogant, [5]it isn't rude, it doesn't seek its own advantage, it isn't irritable, it doesn't keep a record of complaints, [6]it isn't happy with injustice, but it is happy with the truth. [7]Love puts up with all things, trusts in all things, hopes for all things, endures all things . . .

Which verse from 1 Corinthians 13 was the most difficult to act out?

_____

_____

_____

_____

_____

Think about the description of love found in 1 Corinthians 13:4–7. What is one thing that you have learned about love? Write that here:

_____

_____

_____

_____

_____

What happens when only one person in a relationship follows these verses and the other person does the opposite?

_____

_____

_____

_____

The Story of David and Jonathan

The story of Jonathan and David is one of friendship and love. David is well known for his defeat of Goliath when the king of the people was Saul. David was the youngest child of Jesse and was chosen to be the next King of Israel. This story occurs after the story of David and Goliath when David is likely a little bit older.

The main characters of the story are:
- King Saul, a good king who becomes cruel and jealous
- Jonathan, the son of King Saul and the prince of Israel
- Michal, the daughter of King Saul and wife of David
- David, the son of Jesse who lives in the palace with Saul and Jonathan

David was a shepherd and a loyal and brave young man. He even rescued one of his father's sheep from a lion and a bear. He was chosen by the prophet Samuel to be the next king. Normally, the king's son would inherit the throne. Although Jonathan was the prince, he was not chosen to follow his father as king. Once David was chosen, he was sent to live in the palace with King Saul and Jonathan. He became close to King Saul and Jonathan. Jonathan connected in a special way with David, and David grew in favor with the king. Although Saul liked David, Saul often became angry and suspicious of David's loyalty. Over time, Jonathan and David became very close friends.

The story of David and Jonathan is not only beautiful; it embodies a kind of relationship and love that is loyal, respectful, mutual, and committed. The rest of the story proves their relationship was special.

Their story continues in 1 Samuel 18:1–5 *(CEB)*:

[1]As soon as David had finished talking with Saul, Jonathan's life became bound up with David's life, and Jonathan loved David as much as himself. [2]From that point forward, Saul kept David in his service and wouldn't allow him to return to his father's household. [3]And Jonathan and David made a covenant together because Jonathan loved David as much as himself. [4]Jonathan took off the robe he was wearing and gave it to David, along with his armor, as well as his sword, his bow, and his belt. [5]David went out and was successful in every mission Saul sent him to do. So Saul placed him in charge of the soldiers, and this pleased all the troops as well as Saul's servants.

And in 1 Samuel 20:1–42:

[1]David fled from the camps at Ramah. He came to Jonathan and asked, "What have I done? What is my crime? How have I wronged your father that he wants me dead?" [2]Jonathan said to him, "No! You are not going to die! Listen: My father doesn't do anything big or small without telling me first. Why would my father hide this from me? It isn't true!"

[3]But David solemnly promised in response, "Your father knows full well that you like me. He probably said, 'Jonathan must not learn about this or he'll be upset.' But I promise you—on the Lord's life and yours!—that I am this close to death!" "What do you want me to do?" Jonathan said to David. "I'll do it." [5]"Okay, listen," David answered Jonathan. "Tomorrow is the new moon, and I'm supposed to sit with the king at the feast. Instead, let me go and I'll hide in the field until nighttime. [6]If your father takes note of my absence, tell him, 'David begged my permission to run down to his hometown Bethlehem, because there is an annual sacrifice there for his whole family.' [7]If Saul says 'Fine,' then I, your servant, am safe. But if he loses his temper, then you'll know for certain that he intends to harm me. [8]So be loyal to your servant, because you've brought your servant into a sacred covenant with you. If I'm guilty, then kill me yourself; just don't take me back to your father." [9]"Enough!" Jonathan replied. "If I can determine for certain that my father intends to harm you, of course I'll tell you!" [10]"Who will tell me if your father responds harshly?" David asked Jonathan. [11]"Come on," Jonathan said to David. "Let's go into the field." So both of them went out into the field.

[12]Then Jonathan told David, "I pledge by the Lord God of Israel that I will question my father by this time tomorrow or on the third day. If he seems favorable toward David,

I will definitely send word and make sure you know. [13]But if my father intends to harm you, then may the Lord deal harshly with me, Jonathan, and worse still if I don't tell you right away so that you can escape safely. May the Lord be with you as he once was with my father. [14]If I remain alive, be loyal to me. But if I die, [15]don't ever stop being loyal to my household. Once the Lord has eliminated all of David's enemies from the earth, [16]if Jonathan's name is also eliminated, then the Lord will seek retribution from David!" [17]So Jonathan again made a pledge to David because he loved David as much as himself.

[18]"Tomorrow is the festival of the new moon," Jonathan told David. "You will be missed because your seat will be empty. [19]The day after tomorrow, go all the way to the spot where you hid on the day of the incident, and stay close to that mound. [20]On the third day I will shoot an arrow to the side of the mound as if aiming at a target. [21]Then I'll send the servant boy, saying, 'Go retrieve the arrow.' If I yell to the boy, 'Hey! The arrow is on this side of you. Get it!' then you can come out because it will be safe for you. There won't be any trouble—I make a pledge on the Lord's life. [22]But if I yell to the young man, 'Hey! The arrow is past you,' then run for it, because the Lord has sent you away. [23]Either way, the Lord is witness between us forever regarding the promise we made to each other." [24]So David hid himself in the field. When the new moon came, the

king sat at the feast to eat. [25]He took his customary seat by the wall. Jonathan sat opposite him while Abner sat beside Saul. David's seat was empty.

[26]Saul didn't say anything that day because he thought, Perhaps David became unclean somehow. That must be it. [27]But on the next day, the second of the new moon, David's seat was still empty. Saul said to his son Jonathan, "Why hasn't Jesse's son come to the table, either yesterday or today?" [28]Jonathan answered Saul, "David begged my permission to go to Bethlehem. [29]He said, 'Please let me go because we have a family sacrifice there in town, and my brother has ordered me to be present. Please do me a favor and let me slip away so I can see my family.' That's why David hasn't been at the king's table."

[30]At that, Saul got angry at Jonathan. "You son of a stubborn, rebellious woman!" he said. "Do you think I don't know how you've allied yourself with Jesse's son? Shame on you and on the mother who birthed you! [31]As long as Jesse's son lives on this earth, neither you nor your dynasty will be secure. Now have him brought to me because he's a dead man!" [32]But Jonathan answered his father Saul, "Why should David be executed? What has he done?" [33]At that, Saul threw his spear at Jonathan to strike him, and Jonathan realized that his father intended to kill

David. ³⁴Jonathan got up from the table in a rage. He didn't eat anything on the second day of the new moon because he was worried about David and because his father had humiliated him. ³⁵In the morning, Jonathan went out to the field for the meeting with David, and a young servant boy went with him. ³⁶He said to the boy, "Go quickly and retrieve the arrow that I shoot." So the boy ran off, and he shot an arrow beyond him. ³⁷When the boy got to the spot where Jonathan shot the arrow, Jonathan yelled to him, "Isn't the arrow past you?" ³⁸Jonathan yelled again to the boy, "Quick! Hurry up! Don't just stand there!" So Jonathan's servant boy gathered up the arrow and came back to his master. ³⁹The boy had no idea what had happened; only Jonathan and David knew. ⁴⁰Jonathan handed his weapons to the boy and told him, "Get going. Take these back to town."

⁴¹As soon as the boy was gone, David came out from behind the mound and fell down, face on the ground, bowing low three times. The friends kissed each other, and cried with each other, but David cried hardest. ⁴²Then Jonathan said to David, "Go in peace because the two of us made a solemn pledge in the Lord's name when we said, 'The Lord is witness between us and between our descendants forever.'" Then David got up and left, but Jonathan went back to town.

In what way did Jonathan prove to be a trustworthy friend?

_____

_____

_____

_____

_____

What words or phrases in the passage specifically talk about how they care for each other? Go back and highlight or circle these words.

_____

_____

_____

_____

> Jonathan's life became bound up with David's life, and Jonathan loved David as much as himself.
> —1 Samuel 18:1, *CEB*

> And Jonathan and David made a covenant together because Jonathan loved David as much as himself. Jonathan took off the robe he was wearing and gave it to David, along with his armor, as well as his sword, his bow, and his belt.
> —1 Samuel 18:3–4, *CEB*

"What do you want me to do?" Jonathan said to David. "I'll do it.'"
—1 Samuel 20:4, *CEB*

"If I remain alive, be loyal to me. But if I die, don't ever stop being loyal to my household."
—1 Samuel 20:14–15a, *CEB*

So Jonathan again made a pledge to David because he loved David as much as himself.
—1 Samuel 20:17, *CEB*

As soon as the boy was gone, David came out from behind the mound and fell down, face on the ground, bowing low three times. The friends kissed each other, and cried with each other, but David cried hardest.
—1 Samuel 20:41, *CEB*

Think back to our verses from 1 Corinthians 13. What aspects of David and Jonathan's relationship demonstrate that kind of love?

_____

_____

_____

_____

_____

How did David and Jonathan both give and take in their relationship?

_____

_____

_____

_____

_____

What other qualities of true friendship and meaningful love did David and Jonathan exhibit?

_____

_____

_____

_____

_____

How did David and Jonathan show respect for each other?

_____

_____

_____

_____

_____

Friendship

Complete these sentences:

1. Friendship is . . .

_____
_____
_____
_____
_____

2. True friendship feels like . . .

_____
_____
_____
_____
_____

3. Being a friend means . . .

_____
_____
_____
_____
_____

4. Friendships are sometimes hard when . . .

_____

_____

_____

_____

_____

5. A friend . . . *(use verbs—action words)*

_____

_____

_____

_____

_____

YOU ARE RELATIONAL (PART 2)

*Holy God, one who took on flesh and lived as one of us, dwell
with us here and give us courage to learn, grow,
and become more like you—
loving, kind, and full of grace—
through God our Creator, Christ our Redeemer,
and the Spirit our Sustainer. Amen.*

The Story of Ruth and Naomi

This is the story of Ruth, who became the great grandmother of Jesus. These are the main characters:

- *Judah*—a man from Bethlehem
- *Naomi*—wife to Judah, mother to two sons
- *Ruth*—married to one of Naomi's sons
- *Orpah*—married to one of Naomi's sons

During the time when judges ruled in Israel, there was a famine in the land. Judah and his wife Naomi decided to travel to a nearby country called Moab. They took their two sons with them to live in Moab hoping that there would be food and land to farm.

When the sons become adults they married two Moab women. One was named Orpah and the other Ruth. Naomi's husband, Judah, died leaving Naomi alone with her two sons and their two wives. In that culture the sons would be responsible for taking care of their own wives. It was important for women to be married because that relationship kept women safe and protected. When a woman's husband died, her husband's family would take care of her and her children as a way to honor the man who had died. When Judah died, this was very difficult for Naomi, because all she had were her two sons and their wives. Naomi stayed in Moab with her two sons and their wives.

The time and place Ruth and Naomi lived in was much different than today. The rights of women were tied to the men in their lives: their husbands, sons, and fathers. In the story of Ruth and Naomi, we see that they are left without such people. It would not have been possible for them to buy their own home, own land, or start a new way of earning a living apart from their husbands, sons, and fathers.

After about 10 years, Naomi's two sons both died, leaving Orpah and Ruth without husbands to care for them. Naomi had lost her husband and her two sons; she felt very alone.

Naomi wanted leave the country of Moab to go back to Bethlehem because she had heard that there was more food in Bethlehem. Naomi was concerned for her two daughters-in-law, who no longer had husbands. Orpah and Ruth didn't know what to do either. Should they stay with Naomi or go back to their own families?

Ruth 1:8–17, NRSV
[8]Naomi said to her two daughters-in-law, "Go back each of you to your mother's house. May the Lord deal kindly with you, as you have dealt with the dead and with me. [9]The Lord grant that you may find security, each of you in the house of your husband." Ruth and Orpah were both very sad and they cried. [10]They said to her, "No, we will return with you to your people." [11]Naomi replied, "Turn back, my daughters, why will you go with me? Do

I still have sons in my womb that they may become your husbands? [12]Turn back, my daughters, go your way, for I am too old to have a husband. Even if I thought there was hope for me, even if I should have a husband tonight and bear sons, [13]would you then wait until they were grown? Would you then refrain from marrying? No, my daughters, it has been far more bitter for me than for you, because the hand of the Lord has turned against me." [14]Then they wept aloud again. Orpah kissed her mother-in-law, but Ruth clung to her.

[15]So she said, "See, your sister-in-law has gone back to her people and to her gods; return after your sister-in-law." [16]But Ruth said, "Do not press me to leave you or to turn back from following you! Where you go, I will go; Where you lodge, I will lodge; your people shall be my people, and your God my God. [17]Where you die, I will die—there will I be buried. May the Lord do thus and so to me, and more as well, if even death parts me from you!" When Naomi saw that Ruth was determined to stay with her and travel back to the land of Judah, she didn't argue with Ruth anymore.

Work with a partner to answer these questions:

Describe Naomi and Ruth's relationship. Was it love? infatuation? friendship? Explain your choice(s) based on the passage.

_____

_____

_____

_____

_____

How do you think Ruth felt when she was faced with the decision of going home or staying with Naomi?

_____

_____

_____

_____

_____

How do you think Naomi felt when Ruth said she would stay with her?

_____

_____

_____

_____

_____

Did Ruth and Naomi respect one another? Give evidence for your answer.

✏️ _____

_____

_____

_____

Were Ruth and Naomi equals? In other words, did their relationship have equality?

✏️ _____

_____

_____

_____

The definition of *love* is not simple. The scriptures record the relationship between Ruth and Naomi as one that is complex. Just as we learned that we are complex and that David and Jonathan are complex, so are most of the relationships in the Bible—and in real life.

What are some other relationships or stories in the Bible that are complex?

✏️ _____

_____

_____

_____

Situations

Here are 10 total descriptions for you to analyze about love and friendship. Your job is to determine whether the relationship is one of *love, friendship*, or *infatuation*.

#1 Steve and Christine have been noticing each other for several weeks now. They pretend they don't see each other. Finally, Steve called Christine and asked her to be his girlfriend. Christine said yes. After hanging up, Christine texted her friend Julie and told her she was madly in love.

#2 Antonio and Sandra have been going out together for a year. They spend time with each other's families and have even been on a few "real" dates. They like talking to each other and share many common interests. Sometimes they argue, but they keep talking until they have worked things out.

#3 Shawna met Taylor while on vacation at the beach last year. They spent lots of time together during the week at the beach and had a great time. Taylor knows that Shawna is a special person and very sweet, but after returning home from vacation their e-mails and texts became less and less frequent.

#4 Hope and Presley have been dating for 3 months. They see each other at school between classes. In the last week, Hope has felt jealous of and angry with Presley because she talks to other girls too much. Hope texts Presley several times a day to ask her what she is doing.

#5 Tim and Craig seem to always be around each other. They go to the movies together, they are on the same lacrosse team, and spend time at each other's houses on the weekends. They often study together.

#6 Susan and David enjoy all kinds of sports and have known each other for 3 years. They are also in the school band together. They are thinking about getting a part-time job at the same restaurant.

#7 Terry and Sam are neighbors and have known each other for a long time. They used to spend a lot of time together. Lately, they have hung out a couple times a month and sometimes go to the park. When they see other people on the way to the park, they stop and talk to friends and neighbors.

#8 Anna and Meg were in the same homeroom for many years. Something has changed now that they are in fewer classes together. Lately they haven't had anything to talk about.

#9 David sits in front of Amy in most of her classes. David asks Amy about homework and gets some help on group projects from Amy.

#10 Portia and Jose have dated for a while. Recently they have wanted to spend more time together. Sometimes they can't go out because of family commitments or homework. They look forward to seeing each other after school. Last week Portia and Jose had a big fight about whether one of them could go to a party without the other. Although they didn't agree, neither one is mad or angry now.

Knowing the Difference

Deciding whether you are in love, in a healthy friendship, infatuated with someone, or a combination of the three requires you to first know the difference between the three. Though we have read about relationships and talked about relationships, deciding what kind of relationship you are in requires both self-awareness and the help of others.

You don't have to decide if you are in love on your own. You don't have to decide if it is infatuation on your own. You don't have to decide if a friendship is healthy on your own. Talk about your relationships with others who can be honest and open with you. Talk about it with your parents.

You can fill in the blank however you'd like. See what you think of this promise:

We have spent a lot of time together talking and learning. I want for us to consider making a promise to each other as we close. You can fill in the blank however you'd like. See what you think of this promise: *I will try to be the kind of friend that is_____.* When you are ready, write your completion to the sentence here:

_____

_____

_____

_____

_____

Prayer

Gracious and Loving God,
you have blessed us with the gift of friends and family.
We thank you for the love that enfolds and the freedom to be ourselves.
We thank you for those who know the love of friendship,
who are patient in listening,
who sit with us when we cry,
who comfort us in pain,
who celebrate with us in joy,
who laugh with us delight,
who remind us that we are God's children.
Bless our friends with faith, hope, and love.
Amen.

SESSION 6

YOU ARE RESPONSIBLE

Therefore, as a prisoner for the Lord, I encourage you to live as people worthy of the call you received from God. Conduct yourselves with all humility, gentleness, and patience. Accept each other with love, and make an effort to preserve the unity of the Spirit with the peace that ties you together.

—Ephesians 4:1–3, *NRSV*

Holy God, one who took on flesh and lived as one of us,
dwell with us here and give us courage to learn, grow,
and become more like you—
loving, kind, and full of grace—
through God our Creator, Christ our Redeemer,
and the Spirit our Sustainer. Amen.

You Are RESPONSIBLE

Complete these sentences:

- Gifts are . . .

_____
_____
_____
_____
_____

- Love is . . .

_____
_____
_____
_____
_____

- Risk-taking is . . .

_____
_____
_____
_____
_____

- Being safe is . . .

_____
_____
_____
_____
_____

- Responsibility is . . .

_____
_____
_____
_____
_____

Fire is a good analogy for our sexuality and for sex.

Sexuality is a *gift* from God. It is a gift born of *love* and to be used with love, never as manipulation or violence, never casually. Using your sexuality when you are not old enough, is full of *risk* and can be *dangerous*.

Why do you think God created sexuality?

_____
_____
_____
_____
_____

How do we know that we are using the gift of sexuality the right way?

_____
_____
_____
_____
_____

Using our sexuality wisely is another way of being a good steward. Just like we can use fire in a positive way, we can use sexuality in a positive way. What can you do to reduce sexuality's risk and danger?

_____
_____
_____
_____
_____

Think about being a good steward of sexuality. Write something after each of the following prompts:

Being physically safe means . . .

_____
_____
_____
_____
_____

Being smart and knowledgeable means . . .

_____
_____
_____
_____
_____

Being emotionally safe means . . .

_____
_____
_____
_____

Being spiritually ready means . . .

_____
_____
_____
_____
_____

Hopes and Dreams

When we think about the gift of sexuality, we have lots of hopes and dreams. Think about some hopes and dreams you have for one of your friends. Complete this letter, thinking of your friend.

Dear Friend, I hope you know

    that gifts are . . .

_____
_____
_____
_____
_____

that love is . . .

_____

_____

_____

_____

_____

that risk-taking means . . .

_____

_____

_____

_____

_____

that being safe means . . .

_____

_____

_____

_____

_____

and that you are responsible when . . .

_____

_____

_____

_____

_____

Your friend,

_____

_____

_____

_____

_____

By understanding the full range of sexuality and love with a sense of values, you are capable of making responsible and meaningful decisions and to act according to those values.[6]

6 Education for Mission and Ministry Unit. *Sexuality: A Divine Gift* (NY: Domestic and Foreign Missionary Society, 1987), 4.

YOU ARE KNOWLEDGEABLE

Knowledge is powerful and empowering.
[F]or wisdom will come into your heart,and
knowledge will be pleasant to your
soul; prudence will watch over you; and
understanding will guard you.
—Proverbs 2:10–11, *NRSV*

Here are the statements and comments for the Fact and Fiction Game:

1. Most teenagers have had sexual intercourse.	FICTION	While it is true that about half of all teenagers (15–19 years old) have had sexual intercourse, it is also true that about half have not had intercourse.

Percentage of never-married teenagers 15–19 years of age who have ever had intercourse, by age and sex: United States, 2002, 2006–2010, and 2011–2013

Female	2002	2006–2010	2011–2013
15–19 years of age	45.5%	42.6%	44.1%
15–17 years of age	30.3%	27.0%	30.2%
18–19 years of age	68.8%	62.7%	64.4%

Male	2002	2006–2010	2011–2013
15–19 years of age	45.7%	41.8%	46.8%
15–17 years of age	31.3%	28.0%	34.4%
18–19 years of age	64.3%	63.9%	64.0%

Sources:
Vital and Health Statistics
Teenagers in the United States: Sexual Activity, Contraceptive Use, and Childbearing, 2006–2010 National Survey of Family Growth Series 23, Number 31 October 2011

NCHS Data Brief, No. 209, July 2015 U.S. DEPARTMENT OF HEALTH AND HUMAN SERVICES Centers for Disease Control and Prevention National Center for Health Statistics Sexual Activity, Contraceptive Use, and Childbearing of Teenagers Aged 15–19 in the United States Gladys M. Martinez, Ph.D.; and Joyce C. Abma, Ph.D.

2. Once a biologically female person has her first period, she can become pregnant.	FACT	When a person starts having menstrual periods, it means that her reproductive organs have begun working and that she can become pregnant. It does not mean, however, that the body is ready to have a baby. Teen mothers often deliver premature babies. To be ready to have a child involves many aspects, including readiness cognitively, psychologically, spiritually, emotionally, relationally, and economically.
3. For a biologically female person to bathe or swim during her period is unhealthy.	FICTION	There is no reason that someone should restrict any activity during their period.
4. The sperm cell from the male determines the biological sex of a baby.	FACT	The sperm cell provides the genetic message that determines gender.
5. A teenager does not need parental consent to get birth control from a clinic.	FACT & FICTION	Family planning clinics in most states don't have to tell anyone (parents included) in order to provide birth control to teenagers. However, in some states parents do have to give their consent in order for teenagers to get birth control.

(Continued)

6. Sexually transmitted infections (STIs) occur without having any symptoms.	FACT	While some STIs have quite recognizable symptoms, others may not. Gonorrhea and Chlamydia, for example, display no symptoms in females and often are undetectable in males. A doctor's examination is important if a person thinks they may have an STI.
7. If a biologically female person is not menstruating by the time she is 16, there is something wrong.	FICTION	Absolutely not. For a biologically female individual to begin having a period as early as age 8 or as late as 16 or 17 is perfectly normal. If a female is 16 and is worried because she has not yet started menstruating, she can always see a doctor to ensure everything is okay.
8. A biologically female person can get pregnant from sex during her period.	FACT	A biologically female person can get pregnant any time during her menstrual cycle, including during her period.
9. Birth control pills cause cancer.	FICTION	Though side effects can occur from using the pill, there is no conclusive evidence that the pill causes cancer.
10. Only LGBTQ+ (lesbian, gay, bisexual, transgender, queer) people and drug users are at risk for HIV AIDS.	FICTION	While sex between two men and intravenous drug use remain the largest exposure categories, people infected through heterosexual contact comprise the fastest-growing segment of the AIDS population.

11. In order for sperm to be manufactured, the temperature in the testicles must be slightly cooler than normal body temperature, but not too cool.	FACT	Sperm cells can only be manufactured in the testicles when they are slightly cooler than body temperature. The scrota acts like a temperature gauge. When a biologically male body is warm the testicles are allowed to hang away from the body. When it is cold (cold air or cold water), the scrotum draws the testicles up closer to the body to keep them from being too cool.
12. Teenagers can be treated for sexually transmitted infections without their parent's permission.	Depends	Laws vary, but most states require parental permission to provide treatment for STIs to teenagers.
13. Alcohol and marijuana are sexual stimulants.	FICTION	There really are no sexual stimulants. Alcohol and marijuana lessen an individual's inhibitions but they do not stimulate sexual activity.
14. There is one absolutely safe time between menstrual cycles when a biologically female individual cannot get pregnant.	FICTION	Because of the variability of the menstrual and ovulation cycle, the time when the egg is present cannot be determined exactly.

(Continued)

15. Wet dreams happen to every biologically male individual.	FICTION	Some people do not have nocturnal emissions.
16. When a rape occurs, the rapist is usually a stranger.	FICTION	The majority of rapes are perpetrated by someone known to the victim.
17. Once an erection occurs and an individual is excited, without intercourse there can be physical harm.	FICTION	An erection is not actually painful. Erections have occurred since an individual was a fetus. An erection will go away on its own.
18. A person can get pregnant even if a male does not ejaculate or "come" inside of her.	FACT	A person can get pregnant even if their partner "comes" outside of her body. During foreplay, oral sex, or intercourse, semen, which contains sperm, seeps out of the penis.
19. If a person misses a period, they are definitely pregnant.	FICTION	There are many reasons a person might miss a period. Some medications and even exercise can suppress a person's menstrual cycle.

20. You cannot get HIV/AIDS from touching things that a person with HIV/AIDS has used.	FACT	HIV/AIDS is not transmitted by casual contact like sharing drinks, or cups, hugging, kissing, or holding hands.
21. Virginity can be proven.	FICTION	You cannot tell someone's sexual history by looking at them or by engaging in sexual activity, including sexual intercourse.
22. People who start having sexual intercourse before the age of 16 are more likely to get pregnant than those who wait until they are over 18 to have sex.	FACT	People who have sex before they are 16 have a higher rate of pregnancy due to the lack of birth control. Many teenagers are not prepared for sexual intercourse and do not engage in "safer sex."
23. Individuals are born with all of their eggs in their ovaries.	FACT	The eggs inside the ovaries are developed when the person is a fetus inside the mother's uterus. Women do not produce more eggs over their lifetime. Although the eggs are in the ovaries as a baby and child, they are undeveloped.

(Continued)

24. Oral sex is safe because you cannot get pregnant or contract STIs.	FICTION	STIs are transmitted by the touching of genital areas or mouths. Oral sex doesn't protect from STIs. An individual can get pregnant even if the partner "comes" outside of her body. During foreplay, oral sex or intercourse, semen, which contains sperm, seeps out of the penis.
25. There is nothing wrong with looking at pornography.	FICTION	Pornography is sexually-explicit images. Those images are a distortion of God's creation. People in pornography are seen as objects of sexual pleasure and not as children of God. We should strive to behave in such a way that shows respect for all people. Pornography is also addictive; looking at pornography leads people to want to look at more and more sexually-explicit material.
26. Drinking alcohol leads to the same effects for adults and teenagers.	FACT & FICTION	Alcohol is a drug, a legal drug for those 21 and older. Although drinking alcohol is legal for adults and not for teenagers, there are other reasons to avoid alcohol use as a teenager. Because teens are still growing and maturing, the risks and dangers associated with alcohol use are greater for teens than for adults. Drinking alcohol negatively affects an adolescent's growing body and brain. Because teenagers' brains are not fully developed, their impulse control and willingness to delay gratification are not fully developed, which can lead to poor decision-making. In both adults and teens, alcohol hinders decision-making skills and loosens natural inhibitions leading to risky behaviors.

27. Consuming alcohol does not affect decision-making.	FICTION	In both adults and teens, alcohol hinders decision-making skills.
28. Inaccurate as well as accurate information about sexuality can be found on the Internet.	FACT	The Internet can be a good resource for information and it can also provide false or incomplete information. As with any source of information, remember to "consider the source" before you believe something that you read or hear.
29. Masturbation is a normal part of a person's sexuality.	FACT	Although our society used to think that masturbation was "bad," we now know that masturbation is a normal part of sexuality.
30. Drugs and alcohol do not have anything to do with sexual activity.	FICTION	The decision to engage in activity or sexual intercourse is based on judgment. Both alcohol and drugs impair judgment and loosen natural inhibitions. A person who is using alcohol or drugs may find that they do something that they normally wouldn't do, like engage in sexual activity.

Write down three things that you knew before playing the game:

1.

2.

3.

Write down three things that you learned while playing the game:

1.

_____
_____
_____
_____

2.

_____
_____
_____
_____

3.

_____
_____
_____
_____

Write down three things that you'd like to know more about:

1.

_____
_____
_____
_____
_____

2.

_____
_____
_____
_____
_____

3.

_____
_____
_____
_____
_____

Situation Game

Situation 1:

Jordon is a good student and has done well in middle school. Jordon's parents are not sure a 13-year-old should date. Jordon and Liz have been friends for a while and Jordon would like to ask her out on a date. He thinks that a double date with his high-school brother would be perfect. His brother could drive Jordon and Liz.

- What factors and unintended consequences should be considered?
- What should Jordon's parents do?

Situation 2:

John's friends are texting inappropriate pictures, also known as "sexting," to each other. John has tried to tell his friends that they should not send text messages with inappropriate photos, but that just caused them to say rude and mean things about John, to John, and to other people.

- What factors and unintended consequences should be considered?
- What advice would you give John?

Situation 3:

Claire's boyfriend wants her to run track with him. It is not that she thinks girls cannot be athletes; it is that she is not interested. The problem is how to tell him without hurting his feelings.

- What factors and unintended consequences should be considered?
- What should she do?

Situation 4:

Ayana is interested in going out with Demarco, but he has not paid very much attention to her. He is in most of her classes. Her friends say she has to wait until he calls her.

- What factors and unintended consequences should be considered?
- What should she do?

Situation 5:

Jane has arranged to meet three friends at the movies and then go to dinner at a restaurant next to the theater. After meeting her friends, one of the girls suggests walking about a mile to the mall instead of going to the movie and dinner. Jane doesn't think they should walk to the mall. She has tried to tell her friends that she doesn't think it is a good idea.

- What factors and unintended consequences should be considered?
- What should Jane do?

_____

_____

_____

_____

Situation 6:

David was invited to go to the movies with three other guy friends. His parents know the other friends who will be there. When he gets to the theater, he finds out that girls have been invited. David's parents do not want him to go to the movies with girls.

- What are the factors and unintended consequences that should be considered?
- What should he do?

_____

_____

_____

_____

_____

As you grow and learn, you will gain new freedoms and privileges. You will become more independent. With new freedoms and privileges comes greater responsibility.

Sometimes what you want and what your parents want may seem to be opposites. Remember:

- Parents are thinking about your safety.
- Middle-schoolers think about independence.
- Parents like a plan.
- Middle-schoolers like to be spontaneous.
- Parents often see the unexpected consequences.
- Middle-schoolers don't always have the experience to see the consequences clearly.
- Parents want middle-schoolers to grow into their independence.
- Middle-schoolers are sometimes in a hurry to grow up.
- Parents want middle-schoolers to be successful with new freedoms and situations.
- Middle-schoolers want to have FUN!

There are a few things that will help you as you navigate new situations and new freedoms.

- Make a clear plan with your friends and your parents.
- Stick with the plan—don't make last-minute changes to the plan.
- Talk about the new situation with your parents and brainstorm things that you may need to know.
- If you get to an event—or someone's house—and what you thought was the plan is not the plan, call your parents for a ride home. You don't have to stay in a situation in which you feel uncomfortable.

FACT or FICTION

There are lots of FACTS and plenty of FICTION out there about sex. We can say the same thing about our faith. Some would say that God and sex—or faith and sex—don't go together. One of the main goals of these sessions is to prove that this kind of separation is FICTION.

Where is God in the midst of these situations? Situations like the ones you worked on in small groups happen every day in your lives.

What is really cool about the Bible, the book that Christians hold up and use as a guide for life, is that it is filled with similar situations. The authors and people in the stories of the Bible may not have had our technology, but they had our drama!

The following verses from the Bible uplift and remind us that, even in tricky situations, God is always with us. Read these verses:

> [38]For I am convinced that neither death, nor life, nor angels, nor rulers, nor things present, nor things to come, nor powers, [39]nor height, nor depth, nor anything else in all creation, will be able to separate us from the love of God in Christ Jesus our Lord.
> —Romans 8:38–9:5, *NRSV*

> [1]I therefore, the prisoner in the Lord, beg you to lead a life worthy of the calling to which you have been called [2]with all humility and gentleness, with patience, bearing with

one another in love, [3]making every effort to maintain the unity of the Spirit in the bond of peace. [4]There is one body and one Spirit, just as you were called to the one hope of your calling, [5]one Lord, one faith, one baptism, [6]one God and Father of all, who is above all and through all and in all.

—Ephesians 4:1–6, *NRSV*

[10]Do not fear, for I am with you, do not be afraid, for I am your God; I will strengthen you, I will help you, I will uphold you with my victorious right hand.

—Isaiah 41:10, *NRSV*

[27]Peace I leave with you; my peace I give to you. I do not give to you as the world gives. Do not let your hearts be troubled, and do not let them be afraid.

—John 14:27, *NRSV*

[1]God is our refuge and strength, a very present help in trouble. [2]Therefore we will not fear, though the earth should change, though the mountains shake in the heart of the sea.

—Psalm 46:1–2, *NRSV*

Which verse stood out to you? Write your thoughts here:

✏️ _____

_____

_____

_____

All of these words we hear as followers of God the Father, Jesus the Son, and the Holy Spirit our guide. Amen.

A Collect for the Renewal of Life

O God, the King eternal, whose light divides the day from the night and turns the shadow of death into the morning: Drive far from us all wrong desires, incline our hearts to keep your law, and guide our feet into the way of peace; that, having done your will with cheerfulness during the day, we may, when night comes, rejoice to give you thanks; through Jesus Christ our Lord. Amen.[7]

....

7 *Book of Common Prayer*, p. 99.

YOU ARE
CONNECTED

*Holy God, one who took on flesh and lived as one of us, dwell
with us here and give us courage to learn, grow,
and become more like you—
loving, kind, and full of grace—
through God our Creator, Christ our Redeemer,
and the Spirit our Sustainer. Amen.*

Five to Decide

During the Five to Decide Game, you agreed with some things and disagreed with others.

What did you learn about your parents?

_____
_____
_____
_____

What questions surprised you the most?

_____
_____
_____
_____

Interviews

Use active listening skills as you interview your parent. Ask your parent to describe how their faith, community, and family values influence the answers they give:

- How did you learn about sex?
- Did you have sex education or family life education in school?

- Who did you talk to about sexual issues?
- Did you like the way you learned about sexuality?
- What would you have wanted to be different?
- Where do you think your values about sexuality come from? How did you learn them?
- What do you think are appropriate forms of sexual expression for someone my age who identifies as my gender?
- What do you think are appropriate forms of sexual expression for someone the same age as me but identifies as another gender than me?
- When you were my age, to whom were you attracted?
- Now that you are older, how has your attraction to others changed?

Reflect on the experience of interviewing another person. In some ways, I wonder if the interviews you conducted could be compared to a story in the Old Testament, a story of a conversation with God. This story reminds us that a conversation is supposed to include speaking and listening.

In the story of Elijah in 1 Kings 19, Elijah has a conversation with God. The Bible tells us that Elijah had spent the night in a cave—Elijah was feeling very far away from God. The conversation he had with God is beautiful and surprising, because it includes both speaking and listening.

The word of the Lord told Elijah to go outside of the cave and wait for the LORD to pass by (1 Kings 19:11). At first, there was a great wind that split the mountains and broke rocks into pieces (1 Kings 19:11). Then there was an earthquake and then a fire (1 Kings 19:12). In the story we are told that the LORD was not in the wind, the fire, or the earthquake. Finally, the passage says, "And after the fire a sound of sheer silence" (1 Kings 19:12 *NRSV*).

It was in the silence that Elijah came out of the cave and spoke with God.

If you were going to describe your interview today, would you call it a great wind? How about an earthquake? Perhaps a fire?

Describe your interview as one of these three images: *wind, fire*, or *earthquake*. For example, you might say, "My interview was like a *fire* because it _____."

YOU ARE
EMPOWERED

Instead of each person watching out for
their own good, watch out for what
is better for others. Adopt the attitude
that was in Christ Jesus.
—Philippians 2:4-5, *CEB*

Participant Expert Info

Expert Info 1: Refusal Skills

Saying "no" to your friends can be very hard sometimes. You may be afraid of what they will think of you if you don't go along with them. Here are some good ways to say "no" and still be cool.

Say something caring, for example:

- That's flattering but . . .
- It's nice of you to offer, but . . .
- Thanks for asking, but . . .
- I'm glad you trust me to ask, but . . .
- I love you, but . . .
- I like you, but . . .
- I care about you, but . . .
- I'm sure you have a good reason for asking, but . . .

Say what the problem is, for example:

- I am not allowed to do that.
- I disagree with you.
- That is not the plan.

State your decision.

- I'd rather . . .
- I prefer . . .
- I'm going to . . .
- I'm not going to . . .
- I don't believe in . . .

- I've decided not to . . .
- I've decided to . . .

Say what the consequences are.
- I will be grounded.
- It will hurt our friendship.
- This goes against who I am.

Suggest something to do instead.
- Would you like to . . .?
- How about . . .?
- Why not . . . instead?

Options:
- If your friends insist on doing it anyway, leave.
- Try to leave the door open for them to change their minds and join you.
- You don't have to give a reason for your refusal.
- It's okay to state your reason.
- But you never have to give a reason; it only gives the person something to argue about.

Ways to say "no":
- I am uncomfortable with what you are asking.
- That's my phone.
- My parents would kill me.
- It doesn't feel right.

- I don't want to.
- You're crazy.
- Let's get something to eat.
- I feel sick.
- I just want to be friends.
- I want you to leave.
- I am not ready.
- I would rather watch the game.
- Let me think about it.
- Let's go to a movie.
- I said "no" and I mean it!
- I don't know you very well.
- I have to go now.
- It is wrong.
- Don't ask me to make this choice.
- My parents are waiting up.
- Did you hear that?
- Let's stop seeing each other for a while.
- It's not worth it.
- I'm not comfortable.
- I've got homework to do.
- I have a headache.
- You're just using me.
- If you loved me you wouldn't keep asking.
- Don't make me laugh.
- If I were you, I would leave.
- You aren't listening to me.

- I can't take care of a child.
- This isn't what I had in mind.
- It is against my values.
- I'm scared.
- You are hurting my feelings.
- I think I hear my dad.
- The coach said not to.
- I don't want to mess up my hair.
- Not everyone's doing it. I'm not.
- Thanks, anyway.
- I'm too tired.
- I have a game tomorrow.
- It's past my curfew.
- I have to walk the dog.
- I thought you were different.
- Go away.
- Let's think about the consequences.
- I have to go to the bathroom.
- I have to get up early.
- My friends will be here any minute.
- Did you know that I know over 50 ways to say "no"?
- My stuffed animals are watching.
- Take the hint!
- Nada, never.
- I'd be sorry later.
- No!

Expert Info 2: Sex for Sale

If there is a way to make money with sex, somebody is bound to try it.

Prostitution and pornography are two examples. Prostitutes are people—women, men, girls, and boys—who are paid to perform sexual acts. Pornography is any image that exploits sexuality and misuses the gift of sex. Prostitution and pornography turns something intimate and beautiful into something that is bought and sold.

Why would someone become a prostitute?

Like so many reasons that people do things, the answer is complicated. Some prostitutes were abused as children. Some are attracted to the cash income that comes with prostitution; others see it as a way out of poverty, and some report that they would leave prostitution if they could find another job. Some people have been forced by someone more powerful to be prostitutes. We need to be careful not to stereotype people.

The lives of prostitutes are often filled with danger.

Prostitutes are frequently the victims of violence. People who pay to use a prostitute's body seldom care what happens to the prostitute. Often prostitutes are living with people who are involved with illegal drugs and can be addicted to drugs themselves.

People who pay another person for sex can experience negative consequences.

In many cities, local newspapers print the names of people who have been arrested for trying to buy the service of prostitutes. In addition to the legal consequences, people often find their lives ruined by the publicity their actions receive. Prostitution is illegal in most places. It is frequently associated with crimes of violence and drug use.

Jesus was often accused of being seen with prostitutes.

These stories are often illustrations of Jesus's compassion for all people and the difference he could make in the lives of people who had misused the gift of sexuality.

Pornography is any image that exploits human beings and misuses the gift of sexuality.

Everybody at one time or another might be curious enough to look at pictures of naked bodies. Pictures like these are widely available on the Internet or in magazines.

Pornography is any picture or image
- that turns people into sex objects, or
- promotes sexual relations between children and adults, or
- links sex and violence.

Anytime you see people or sexuality being exploited, or used as a way to make money, you are probably looking at pornography. Pornography is addictive, so it is easy to sell once a person's normal curiosity gets "hooked."

Pornography is often found on the Internet. If you see pictures or get onto a website that you know shows pornography, tell you parents immediately.

Expert Info 3: Assertive vs. Aggressive

Assertive behavior is a healthy, positive way of expressing your own needs.

Aggressive behavior is an unhealthy way of getting your way by attacking others.

Aggressive behavior is about getting the other person to do what you want them to do in a forceful or violent way. Aggressive behavior can include yelling, screaming, hitting, biting, kicking, slamming doors, and pushing. Behaviors like rape, physical attack, assault, and shooting are more serious forms of aggression that are illegal.

More common forms of aggression that you might experience include:

- yelling, threatening, or frightening others
- spreading rumors
- gossiping (talking about other people), spreading rumors (telling stories about other people)
- creating or participating in groups that exclude others, and influencing others to reject other people

Why are some people aggressive?

People your age sometimes act aggressively because that is how they have learned to act; it can be a learned behavior.

Sometimes young people have a hard time expressing their real feelings of pain, hurt, shame, or loneliness, and they use aggressive behavior to protect themselves. Some people have more complex signs of mental illness or of emotional disabilities and need the help of doctors, psychologists, and counselors.

Often, aggressive behavior is called *bullying*. Bullying can describe a wide range of behavior that harms other people. Bullying and aggressive behavior may lead to the person getting what they want in the short term, but over a longer period of time, these negative and destructive behaviors hurt their relationships.

Advantages of being assertive

Being assertive is a practice of standing up for yourself by using words and being honest about your feelings and emotions. Learning to express your own needs takes practice, but is worth the extra effort. Relationships benefit from assertive behavior that respects the interests and rights of other people. Assertive people have good interpersonal skills; they speak up when they see injustice, and they develop strong decision-making skills. Most importantly, they learn more about themselves and learn to treat others with the respect that every person deserves. In being assertive, you are demonstrating self-confidence, self-respect, and the ability to stand up for yourself effectively.

More common forms of assertive behavior that you might experience include:
- listening to other people
- respecting the thoughts and feeling of others

- making "I" statements when making requests
- using *When . . ., I feel* statements: When you do _____, I feel _____.
- being firm without attacking the other person

In our faith life, we have good examples of people who were assertive. Jesus, Martin Luther King, Jr., and Mother Teresa all stood up for what they believed and influenced others to do the same. They did not put others down or attack people to make themselves feel stronger.

Expert Info 4: STIs (Sexually Transmitted Infections)

How are STIs passed from person to person?

Sexually Transmitted Infections or STIs are passed from one person to another through sexual contact. There are more than 20 different STIs. Some of the infections that you might hear about are:

- syphilis
- gonorrhea
- chlamydia
- genital herpes

Some STIs can be treated and cured. Others are incurable, meaning that people will have the disease for life and continue to be able to pass it along to others.

What are symptoms commonly associated with STIs?

- unusual discharge (leaking of thick fluid) from the penis or vagina

- irritation, lumps or sores on or around the genitals
- pain or tenderness in the genitals, genital area, or abdomen
- painful urination or frequent need to urinate

A person can have an STI and have no symptoms at all. Because many STIs do not have any symptoms at all, it is common for people to be infected and not be aware that they can pass on an infection. These symptoms can also indicate the presence of other diseases—diseases that are not sexually transmitted. However, people who are sexually active and have any of these symptoms are advised to see their doctor immediately.

How do you get STIs?
- Through sexual conduct: In order to pass the infection from one body to another, two people must make direct contact in a place on the body where STIs typically survive. This kind of contact generally happens during sexual activity.
- Through touching a "survival place": The germs that cause STIs need proper conditions to survive. Places on the body that are warm and moist, such as the penis, vulva, rectum, or mouth provide "survival places" for STIs.

Understand that germs live and die. Most STI germs die soon after they leave the body when they are exposed to air. It is unusual for STI to spread in ways other than human-to-human contact.

Responsible sexual behavior is the best prevention for STIs. For young people, responsible sexual behavior means waiting until you are much older to become sexually active.

Expert Info 5: Tech Talk

Bullying and aggressive behavior using technology is sometimes called *cyber bullying*. Cyber bullying is when people use technology like texting, e-mailing, and posting on social media sites to share offensive or hurtful pictures or comments about other people.

Most young people will be a victim of cyber bullying. These are some of the ways that people might bully others using technology:

- send or text hurtful words or pictures
- post false or misleading stories to embarrass or ridicule others
- forward or share personal information without permission
- pretend they are other people online to trick others
- spread lies and rumors about victims
- trick people into revealing personal information
- send or forward mean text messages
- post pictures of victims without their consent

What should a person do if they are a victim of cyber bullying?

If you have been cyber bullied, save the messages and or pictures to show a trustworthy adult. Young people should let a trusted adult know that they are being cyber bullied—a parent, a teacher, a counselor, or law enforcement officer. Young people need help in stopping the bullying.

Stay safe online:
- Do not forward offensive or inappropriate messages or images.
- Block people who share inappropriate images or words.
- Report cyber bullying to an adult.
- Never meet anyone in person who you only know online.
- Don't share personal information about yourself, your friends or your parents online.

Stay smart online:
- Never post or share offensive or inappropriate images or messages.
- Remember the grandmother test: If you would not want your grandmother to see what you are posting, don't post it!
- Though the Internet can feel private, it is actually very public. Never fall into the trap of believing that what you do online can only be seen by the select few friends on your list.

Expert Info 6: Birth Control

Birth Control is an easy method used to prevent pregnancy. Birth control is not 100% effective, although some methods are more effective than others.

Abstinence

Abstinence is also called *celibacy* or *"saying no."* It is the most effective way to not become pregnant. When it is used to prevent pregnancy, abstinence means not having sexual intercourse (not putting the penis in the vagina) and not ejaculating near the opening of the vagina. In order to protect against sexually transmitted infections (STIs), people would abstain from all sexual activity while using this method.

Condoms

Condoms are like thick strong gloves. A condom is worn over the penis to catch the sperm so they can't enter the uterus and fallopian tubes. Condoms can be bought in a drugstore. They can only be used once then thrown away. Condoms are the only birth control that protects against contracting STIs (other than abstinence). Although condoms are effective in reducing the likelihood that an infection would be passed from one person to another, they are not 100% effective.

The Shot

Also known as Depo-Provera or "depo," the shot is made of hormones. It is given into a woman's muscle (in her arm or hip) and lasts three months. It keeps her ovaries from releasing eggs. A healthcare provider must prescribe the shot. The woman needs to get a shot every 12 weeks.

Pills

Oral contraceptives, often called "the pill," are hormones (like the ones already in her body) that keep a woman's ovaries from releasing eggs as long as she keeps taking them. A healthcare provider must prescribe them. The woman takes one pill by mouth at the same time every day (not just when she has intercourse).

IUDs

IUD stands for Intra-uterine Device. An IUD is a device that is implanted into the female's uterus in the doctor's office. This a reversible type of contraception that does not require daily medication.

The Implant

The Implant, also known as Implanon, is one small tube that is placed under the skin of a woman's upper, inner arm. It prevents pregnancy for up to 3 years by releasing a hormone that prevents her ovaries from releasing eggs. A healthcare provider must prescribe it. The woman must go to her healthcare provider's office to have it put in or removed which only takes a few minutes.

Combining Two Methods

For extra protection, couples can combine a condom with another method of birth control (for example: birth control pills). A combination like this will help cut down the risk of pregnancy, HIV, and many other sexually transmitted infections (STIs).

Safer Sex

Many middle-schoolers have heard of safe sex, but may not know what that means. There really isn't any form of sex or sexual activity that is free from *risk*. The term *safer sex* is the preferred and more accurate term. Safer sex means that a couple has used protection against both pregnancy and STIs. Safer sex means using a condom to protect from STIs along with an effective birth control method, like an oral contraceptive ("the pill") or the depo shot. Some people think that safe sex refers to any sexual activity that cannot lead to pregnancy, like oral sex. It is not true that oral sex is safer than vaginal sex. Oral sex poses health risks as well; STIs can be spread by oral sex.

Jeopardy

Think about the jeopardy game and respond to the following:

What are your favorite ways to say "no"?

_____

_____

_____

_____

_____

Write a scenario that uses three ways to say "no."

✏️ _____

_____

_____

_____

What have you learned about prostitution and pornography? How will this new information inform your decisions in the future?

✏️ _____

_____

_____

_____

What skills do you want to work on in terms of being assertive?

✏️ _____

_____

_____

_____

When you think about technology in your life, what will you do differently after this session?

_____
_____
_____
_____
_____

Describe three situations where you have the power to make wise choices.

_____
_____
_____
_____
_____

SESSION 10

YOU ARE
THOUGHTFUL

Do not be conformed to this world, but be
transformed by the renewing of your
minds, so that you may discern what
is the will of God—what is good and
acceptable and perfect.
—Romans 12:2, *NRSV*

O heavenly Father, who hast filled the world with beauty: Open our eyes to behold thy gracious hand in all thy works; that, rejoicing in thy whole creation, we may learn to serve thee with gladness; for the sake of him through whom all things were made, thy Son Jesus Christ our Lord.[8]

You Are THOUGHTFUL

What are some of the things that you think are inappropriate for you?

_____
_____
_____
_____
_____

What faith, community, or family values are important to you?

_____
_____
_____
_____
_____

8 *Book of Common Prayer*, For Joy in God's Creation, p. 814.

Why would God care if I make appropriate decisions about my life?

✏️ _____

_____

_____

_____

_____

Why would my parents care if I make appropriate decisions about my life?

✏️ _____

_____

_____

_____

_____

A Final Prayer

Our God and our families care because they love us. God loves you unconditionally. God wants what is best in your life and what will make you most fulfilled.

Grant to us, Lord, we pray, the spirit to think and do always those things that are right, that we, who cannot exist without you, may by you be enabled to live according to your will;

*through Jesus Christ our Lord, who lives and reigns with you
and the Holy Spirit, one God, for ever and ever. Amen.*[9]

The Lord bless you and keep you.
Amen.

*The Lord make his face to shine upon you and
be gracious to you.*
Amen.

*The Lord lift up his countenance upon you
and give you peace.*
Amen.

....

9 *Book of Common Prayer*, 232.

GLOSSARY

abortion: A medical procedure to end a pregnancy.

abstinence: A decision to not do what a person wants to do; also called celibacy or "saying no"; sexual abstinence is choosing not to engage in sexual activity.

abuse: To abuse something is to use it in an improper or destructive way.

adolescence: The period in human growth and development that occurs after childhood and before adulthood, from ages 10 to 19. Rapid and significant period of human development.

agape: Unconditional love of the other.

agender: An adjective describing a person who is internally ungendered or does not feel a sense of gender identity.

aggressive behavior: An unhealthy way of getting your way by attacking others; forceful or violent acts; can include yelling, screaming, hitting, biting, kicking, slamming doors, and pushing. More serious forms of aggression that are illegal include rape, physical attack, assault, and shooting.

AIDS: Abbreviation for acquired immunodeficiency syndrome; a disease caused by a virus that can be transmitted from an infected person to an uninfected person only by an exchange of blood, semen, vaginal mucus, urine, or feces; type of sexually transmitted infection.

asexual: An adjective describing people who form meaningful emotional and spiritual connections, but do not experience sexual attraction to others.

assertive behavior: A healthy, positive way of expressing your own needs.

assigned sex: Gender assigned at birth based on biological anatomy.

attraction: When someone is physically drawn to another person or sees someone as desirable.

Baptismal Covenant, the: In The Episcopal Church, the promises made between God, the baptized, and God's people during the liturgy of Holy Baptism. The promises require that we renounce Satan, repent of our sins, and accept Jesus as our Lord and Savior as well as answer other questions with, "I will with God's help." For infants, their parents and sponsors make promises to support the baptized in their journey within the Church, to know Christ, and be able to follow him.

biological sex: The physical anatomy, genetic make-up, and hormones of an individual's body; refers to the physical anatomy of an individual's body at birth.

birth control: Any method used to prevent pregnancy, including, but not limited to: condoms, IUDs, birth control pills, the rhythm method, vasectomy, and tubal ligation.

body image: The way you see yourself, imagine how you look, and feel about your body.

breast: Milk-producing organ on female chest.

circumcision: An operation during which a doctor removes the foreskin of the penis.

cisgender: An adjective describing a person who by nature or by choice conforms to gender-based expectations of society.

clitoris: Small, cylinder-shaped organ located just above the urethra made of very sensitive tissue.

condoms: A sheath worn over the penis to catch the semen during ejaculation; a form of birth control; can reduce the risk of contracting HIV/AIDS.

covenant: A contract or agreement, such as between God and God's people. The New Covenant refers to the new relationship with God given by Jesus Christ, the Messiah, to the apostles, and, through them, to all who believe in him (*BCP* p. 850).

cyber bullying: Bullying and aggressive behavior using technology like texting, e-mailing, and posting to share offensive or hurtful pictures or comments about other people.

combining two methods: To use two methods of birth control together, for example, the birth control pill and condoms.

complexity of sexuality: Understanding that sexuality is understood on a continuum; includes the perspective of biological, sex, gender, sexual orientation, and expression working together to form a complex view of sexuality.

contraception: A couple may use to prevent conception during intercourse and avoid pregnancy.

desire: The urge or instinct that can be sexual when focused on sexual intercourse with another person.

ejaculation: Sudden pushing and squeezing action that forces semen from the penis during male orgasm.

erection: Process by which the blood rushes into the penis causing it to enlarge and stiffen.

fact: A statement that can be proven by science, medicine, and modern research.

faith connection: Both implicit and explicit messages that model to participants how our faith intersects with our sexuality.

fiction: Popular misconception or rumor based on something other than fact, science, and modern research.

flirting: A playful behavior intended to arouse sexual interest or to make playfully romantic or sexual overtures.

friendship: The connecting bond of affection between people. Friendship includes loyalty, respect, mutuality, and commitment.

fruitfulness: To bear fruit; to multiply; plays with the images of God's work of creation. Fruitfulness in Genesis is that manifestation of love that bears witness to the love of God for all creation through Christ.

gay: A person who is attracted to a person of the same sex often calls themself *gay* or *homosexual*.

gender: A socially-determined way of describing human beings based on characteristics like appearance, dress, reproductive organs, and behavior, now thought of as a continuum or spectrum.

gender as binary: The idea that gender is either exclusively male or female, without any room for variation and ambiguity. Excludes many individuals, all of whom are created in the image of God.

gender expression: The way a person interprets their gender with outward displays of that gender stereotype.

gender fluid: An internal sense that someone does not feel like they fit in a specific category for gender. Describes someone who moves in and out different ways of expressing and identifying oneself.

gender identity: Built upon what an individual senses internally about their own gender.

genetic makeup: Refers to whether scientific tests determine a person has xx, xy, or another makeup of chromosomes.

gender roles: Society's set of roles, values, and expectations for what it means to be a girl/woman or a boy/man in a particular culture. Gender roles vary from culture to culture and over time. The United States culture recognizes two distinct gender roles. One is the "masculine" (having the qualities of characteristics attributed to males). The other is the "feminine" (having the qualities or characteristics attributed to females). In other words, this is what we learn from our culture about what a "real man" or a "real woman" is supposed to be/do. A third gender role, rarely condoned in our society, is androgyny, combining assumed male *(andro)* and female *(gyne)* qualities. Note: There are also gender roles around non-binary genders.

genderqueer: An adjective used to describe a person who is part of a group of people who do not feel that they fit into the traditional two genders of a gender-binary system. As with any other group that aligns with transgender identities, the reasons for identifying as genderqueer vary.

heterosexuality: People who are attracted to people of other genders often call themselves *heterosexual* or *straight*.

HIV: human immunodeficiency virus; the virus that leads to AIDS; commonly referred to as HIV/AIDS.

homosexuality: Romantic attraction, sexual attraction, or sexual behavior between members of the same sex or gender. A woman who is attracted to other women often calls herself *gay*, *lesbian*, or *homosexual*. A man who is attracted to other men often calls himself *gay* or *homosexual*.

hormones: Testosterone, progesterone, and estrogen are hormones connected to human sexuality.

hospitality: To welcome and love the stranger as you would your own family.

image: Likeness, semblance.

Imago Dei: "Image of God," denoting the symbolic relation between God and humanity.

"the implant": A tube that is placed under the skin of the upper, inner arm. It prevents pregnancy for up to 3 years by releasing a hormone that prevents the ovaries from releasing eggs. Must be prescribed by a health care provider (a doctor or nurse practitioner). Also known as Implanon.

inclusive language: Language that seeks to include all people, rather than only a few.

infatuation: Immature and fleeting attraction between people.

intersex: An adjective describing someone born with chromosomes, external genitalia, or internal reproductive systems that do not fall into socially-constructed ways of thinking about biological sex (for example, male and female).

IUD: Abbreviation for intra-uterine device; a reversible type of birth control. A device that is implanted into the uterus in the doctor's office.

knowledge: General understanding or familiarity with a principle or term gained through experience or learning.

lesbian: A woman who is attracted to other women

LGBTQ+: The acronym for *Lesbian, Gay, Bisexual, Transgender, Queer, Questioning, Intersex, Asexual*. An inclusive term that seeks to capture all sexual and gender identities other than heterosexual. This is an evolving term, as our understanding and language around sexuality expands and matures.

love: A mature love includes acceptance, non-judgment, and a commitment to help another person grow emotionally and spiritually; respects the dignity of another person; a deep, tender, ineffable feeling of affection toward a person. Love arises in families, in friendships, and through a sense of underlying oneness.

lust: feeling of intense desire and attraction toward a person; the emotion of sex and sexual desire.

masturbation: Touching, rubbing, or stimulating one's own sex organs, producing a pleasurable feeling and sexual excitement.

menstruation: Stage of female menstrual cycle when the inner lining of the uterus is shed and small amount of bloody tissue leaves the body through the vagina.

miscarriage: Ending of a pregnancy.

nocturnal emission: Ejaculation of semen from the penis while male is sleeping. Another name for this is *wet dream*. Only about a teaspoon of semen is released from the penis during ejaculation.

orgasm: The pleasurable and intense release of tension built up as sexual excitement.

ovaries: Glands where female reproductive cells are formed and where hormones are produced. The ovaries release an egg each month that travels down the fallopian tubes toward the uterus.

pangender: An adjective describing a person whose gender identity if made up of all or many gender expressions.

physical anatomy: The structure of the human body. Includes terms relevant to sexuality like penis, ovaries, vagina, and testicles.

penis: Cylinder-shaped organ that consist of a head or glans (which is the most sensitive part) and a shaft of soft spongy tissue.

petting: Any touching of sex organs other than intercourse.

"the pill": An oral contraceptive, often called "the pill." Hormones (like the ones already in a woman's body) that keep the ovaries from releasing eggs as long as she keeps taking them.

pornography: Any image that exploits sexuality and misuses the gift of sex sexuality.

prostitute: A person who is paid to perform sexual acts.

puberty: Time in a young person's life when the body goes from being a child's body to an adult's body. The body becomes able to reproduce. The period of time when pre-teens' and teenagers' bodies change and when the sex organs become capable of reproduction.

pubic hair: Coarse, curly hair that grows in the genital area.

questioning: To be unsure or less certain of your sexual orientation. You can also question your gender identity. People figure out their sexuality and gender identity at different points in their lives, and there's no wrong way to identify.

rape: To force another person to submit to sex acts is a crime, called *rape*.

sexual intercourse: Placement of the penis inside the vagina.

"the shot": Also known as *Depo-Provera* or *Depo*. A type of female birth control given into the muscle (in the arm or hip) and lasting three months. Keeps the ovaries from releasing eggs.

refusal skills: The ability and learned techniques to assertively say "no" to sexual advances.

romantic attraction: Attraction that makes people desire romantic contact or interaction with another person or persons.

romantic orientation: Describes an individual's pattern of romantic attraction based on a person's gender(s) regardless of one's sexual orientation. For individuals who experience sexual attraction, their sexual orientation and romantic orientation are often in alignment; they experience sexual attraction toward individuals of the same gender(s) as the individuals with whom they are interested in forming romantic relationships.

safer sex: the concept of reducing risk in sexual activity by using both condoms and birth control to protect from STI and pregnancy.

sexuality: A great gift from God; ". . . a central aspect of being human throughout life encompasses sex, gender identities and roles, sexual orientation, eroticism, pleasure, intimacy, and reproduction. Sexuality is experienced and expressed in thoughts, fantasies, desires, beliefs, attitudes, values, behaviors, practices, roles, and relationships. While sexuality can include all of these dimensions, not all of them are always experienced or expressed. Sexuality is influenced by the interaction of biological, psychological, social, economic, political, cultural, legal, historical, religious and spiritual factors."[10]

sexual attraction: Attraction that makes people desire sexual contact or show sexual interest in another person.

sexual harassment: A feeling of intense annoyance caused by being tormented. This tormenting is caused by continued unwanted contact and attention or persistent attacks and criticism.

sexual intercourse: Sexual activity between two people, especially penetration of the vagina, anus, or mouth.

sexual orientation: A person's emotional, romantic, and sexual attraction to individuals of a particular gender (male or female). Sexual orientation involves a person's feelings and sense of identity; it may or may not be evident in the person's appearance or behavior. People may have attractions to people of the same or opposite sex, but may elect not to act on these feelings.

scrotum: Soft muscle pouch containing and protecting the testicles.

skill: An ability to perform a task gained through experience or learning—a specific ability.

sperm: Male reproductive cells manufactured by the testicles and ejaculated in the semen. These cells enter the female egg and begin the fertilization process.

....

10 WHO, 2006a www.who.int/topics/sexual_health/en/.

teasing: To annoy or make fun of someone persistently or to arouse hope, desire, or curiosity in another without affording satisfaction.

temptation: The desire to have or do something you know you should avoid.

testicles: In males, the glands that produce hormones and sperm.

uterus: Hollow organ located inside the women's body in the lower abdomen, shaped and sized like an upside-down pear.

vagina: A soft muscular tube about 3" long that makes a passageway from the uterus to the outside of the body; this opening is very stretchy and expands to become the birth canal when a baby is born.

virgin: A person who has never had sexual intercourse. This term can be applied to both males and females.

vulnerability: Emotionally opening ourselves up to each other people.

vulva: Name for the female genitals located between the legs; this name is the general name for the entire female genital area.

womb: Refers to the uterus; often found in the Bible.